LOW

Chrissy Williams is a poet, editor and tutor based in London. Her work has been featured by the BBC and her first collection *BEAR* (Bloodaxe Books, 2017) was one of the *Telegraph*'s 50 Best Books of the Year. The author of numerous pamphlets, her work has been shortlisted for the Michael Marks Award, and published in many magazines and anthologies including *Poetry*, *Poetry Review*, *Poetry London* and Salt's *Best British Poetry* series. Her second book-length collection, *LOW*, was published by Bloodaxe in 2021.

She is editor of the online poetry journal *PERVERSE*, and previously worked both at the National Poetry Library and as director of the Poetry Book Fair. She is also an improviser and edits comics, including the *New York Times* bestselling *The Wicked + The Divine*.

CHRISSY WILLIAMS

LOW

BLOODAXE BOOKS

ISBN: 978 1 78037 564 9

First published 2021 by
Bloodaxe Books Ltd,
Eastburn,
South Park,
Hexham,
Northumberland NE46 1BS.

www.bloodaxebooks.com
For further information about Bloodaxe titles
please visit our website and join our mailing list
or write to the above address for a catalogue

Supported using public funding by
**ARTS COUNCIL
ENGLAND**

Printed in Great Britain by Bell & Bain Limited, Glasgow, Scotland, on
acid-free paper sourced from mills with FSC chain of custody certification.

for Kieron

ACKNOWLEDGEMENTS

Thank you to the editors of the following publications, in which some of these poems were previous published: *Poetry*, *Poetry London, Poetry Wales, The Pussy Parlour, The Rialto*, *Fuselit* and *Long Poem Magazine*, as well as *Tears in the Fence*, *Copper Nickel* and *Where Rockets Burn Through* (Penned in the Margins 2012), in which some early extracts from 'LIEBE' first appeared under different titles.

Thank you to the commissioners of the following events and projects, for which some of these poems were originally created: Poetry for Sonic Youth, the Aldeburgh English Song Project, BBC Free the Word for National Poetry Day and Poem Brut.

Thank you to the various poetry groups I was part of while these poems were being written, for their feedback, community, cats and wine. Thank you to the early readers of this manuscript for their comments and encouragement: Anna Selby, Richard Scott, Matthew Saxton, Lorraine Mariner and Kathryn Maris. Thank you especially to Edward Doegar and Joey Connolly, not just for their invaluable and detailed poetic insights, but for their support on all the other stuff that happens around the poems.

Thank you also to Kieron, but that has nothing to do with poetry.

CONTENTS

on lipsyncing || for || your || life

if i really had to lipsync || for my death || i would be
   screaming every word || just think || your final song
and you don't get to choose it || for yourself || someone else
   critiques || someone else's audience from hell || and
if they give you something difficult || the world might fall away
   just because you never learnt || to be fierce || to fake it
till you make it || maybe || that's where i've gone wrong
   not pretending hard enough || performing || who i want to be
oblivion || don't think oblivion || for faltering || to Kesha
   think oblivion || for botched death drops || from 10,000 feet
fail big || don't fail at home || fail as publicly as possible || pose
   for your final selfie || imagine || dancing to a funeral march
the lord's prayer || your family's favourite hymns || you know
   i stopped mouthing words || in church || years ago

I

The body is good business.

GANG OF FOUR, *'Natural's Not In It'*

! katya !

i want ! to be friends ! with katya ! i want
to dress ! how i want to dress ! like a gale !
full of glitter ! and back alleys ! a seagull
laugh ! to shake our being ! whose secret lies !
perhaps ! in kicking legs upwards in delight !
painted ! an omnivorous harpy ! *goofy* !
loving our friends ! lighting up around them !
what a man ! *unstoppable* ! they'll say, why !
they're the perfect woman ! (now that's me !)
judy jetson ! enraged ! with a penis ! and
obsessed with *Contact* too ! in every situation !
a little Jodie Foster ! *o dear role model*
for my role model ! find meaning ! play parts !
everything real ! happens ! *behind* the eyes !
all those things we cannot prove ! like love !
like the world ! is just ! what we make of it

the / perfect / woman

a new drag / a brash style
of self-declaration / hip-pads
tit-tape / big love / reflecting me
back to me / via a tv screen
via a man / what it means / words
what do words mean / incitement
to / from / femininity / for a self
by implication / a dedicated self
who gets to say / what a woman is
it is not / binary / it's not even
necessary / no rules / no bicycles
my parents' fears / gone / the known
dressed as / the amazing / and me
a fan of / curiosity / whose competition
is this / whose culture / is left out
of this / flawed consumerism / delight
gender / as allusion / as freedom
green eyeliner / everyone / sharing time
the difficult joy / in just / being

Bobbie Gentry, Shangri-Las, Sonic Youth

I

Bobbie Gentry was twenty-five when she wrote 'Fancy'.
Fancy is a girl whose mother buys her a red dress,
a red dancing dress, and sends her out to sell her body.
This work turns out to be something Fancy enjoys
but her enjoyment is measured against her sense of obligation.

'Here's your one chance, Fancy, don't let me down'

II

At sixteen The Shangri-Las sang 'Give Him a Great Big Kiss'
and the kiss was represented with sound <mwa> and a gesture.
'Is he bad?' asks the song, *'Hmm, he's goodbad. He's not evil.'*
There are no mothers in this song. It's just the girls
and Mary's description of dancing with a boy is rapture:

'We were close…very very…close'

III

Kim Gordon sings with Kim Deal on *Washing Machine*,
Sonic Youth's album-as-machine for early sexualisation.
This sexualisation is at its best in 'Little Trouble Girl'
where the Shangri Las' line is poached and sung by women
(if there are bad girls, so there must be bad women):

'Close…very very…close'

IV

I listened to these songs a long time after puberty,
around the time I started having sex. Urgent, always fumbling,
never planning...DESIRE...to be...DESIRE...
collapsing further DESIRE, and more, both before & after.
Quiet now. Something is getting broken.

'Close...very very...close'

V

In the Sonic Youth, Kim transforms the Shangri-Las' line,
acknowledging the way things really change, and how mother
and a sense of obligation to win her love are not the aim.
How past intimacy can be replaced. Fight DESIRE with fire.
How past intimacy can never really be replaced.

'Remember mother? We were close...very very...close'

VI

I allowed my lust to diminish her and I ask forgiveness.
I never wanted to be killed with kindness. I was afraid of love.
I think you will love me only if I am good. The girls sing.
I think you will love me only if I am good. *And if I'm bad?*
The long kiss. The pull of any part of any body. *And if I'm goodbad?*

'Close...very very...close'

17

VII

This is the DESIRE I backed myself into,
the DESIRE I have always been running away from
& all I am now, heart, is DESIRE and soon there will be nothing,
ash & DESIRE, DESIRE & bones & nothing, *so...*
close... this DESIRE
to be good

Tangled

Mother knows best Listen to your mother It's a scary world out there The Eurotunnel Le Shuttle is the fastest route to France by car and adventure is only 35 minutes away I thought I was doing a good job with my normal toothbrush but my dentist said no he told me I should Go Pro with Oral B Jude Law hands me some car keys in Cannes the all new Lexus RX amazing in motion I want skincare that defies ageing without spending ages searching Olay Total Effects your best beautiful Okay Google what's the quickest way home by bike you have reached your destination Walt Disney World Resort Florida a land of neverending wonder where dreams come true and that's just the beginning For the first time in forever I'm completely free I am a horrible daughter I am never going back

poem = sorry

I apologise,
pull out a sigh,

nod, make my face
a gracious lie.

Be nice, in the moment,
a Cheshire smile, or else

fill your self with bees.
Set it on fire.

Beating Face

I am clown realness

BIANCA DEL RIO

The phrase 'to fix my face'.
Sticks and stones. To please.
Face up to. Policing. No
hard angles. Squaring up.
I never forget a face.

Alyssa, what's your secret?
Alyssa blinks. 'I'm a man.'
John Wayne Gacy as a clown,
all terror and triangles. *It.
Dynasty*. A 1980s face.

She gives great face.
Face your worst fears.
Face-to-face at last.
Vulnerable when beautiful.
Face on. *Face Off.*

First makeup, a gift
from mother. Playtime.
The man with 1,000 faces.
The face that launched 1,000
fists. Pouting in cheekbones.

'It's not personal, it's drag.'
The woman in the exfoliating mask.
You beat your face.
I beat mine. Love, love.
Who beats it best?

Signing Off

(for Karen and Georgia on My Favourite Murder*)*

Stay sexy and don't get murdered by a weird mortician!

Stay sexy and don't cut someone's neck with a sword!

Stay sexy and wash your hands well after handling body parts!

Stay sexy and don't let your dog get murdered!

Stay sexy and when in doubt declare your family dead to escape a communist regime!

Stay sexy and don't get in the hot tub as they are already dirty enough and you never know if someone's died in it!

Stay sexy and don't stop by creepy old men's houses on your way home from school!

Stay sexy and especially don't trust anyone with a piano tie!

Stay sexy and always carry a golf club!

Stay sexy and don't run alone at night!

Stay sexy and don't join bowling leagues with killer clowns!

Stay sexy and don't date men who are trying to kill you!

Stay sexy and remember men are always trying to kill you!

Stay sexy and know 90% of murdered women are killed by someone they know, 50% in their own home, and two-thirds by a former or current partner!

Stay sexy and don't get murdered!

II

Though our bodies recoil from the grip of the soil –
Why the long face?

JOANNA NEWSOM, *'Sawdust & Diamonds'*

Joke

WOMAN in hospital bed, DOCTOR operating ultrasound scanner

D: It's confirmed – you're having a joke.

W: I can't believe it! I've enjoyed comedy for years but was so scared of having my own joke!

D: It is rather astounding. Which sketch fathered it?

W: I was in Edinburgh. I saw so many shows. My favourites were all by women and –

D: Appalling. You won't go far without a – Hang on… [*examines monitor, scans her again*]. Ah, don't worry, the joke's on me. It's gone.

W: What do you mean? It's…just…gone?

D: Here, I'll prove it. [*leans over to speak into the woman's stomach*] Knock, knock.

[*long pause*]

See?

Nothing.

Invisible Days

I was pregnant seven times [...] I lost them all

JOAN CRAWFORD in *Mommie Dearest*

it's those early invisible days
when no one knows anything
and everything is possible

after the loss
the unexpected loss
you wish the air would run away

take away the endless chatter
of internal dialogue *Christina*
bring me the axe

there but for the grace of *no wire hangers*
there but for the grace of melodrama
I don't know how to do this without humour

remember those early invisible days
when everything is possible
and I feel inexplicably like my best self
for a short while

Voyage to the Copier Room

A woman struggles with frogspawn onto the 43 this morning.
She is slim, grateful, agrees it is later than she thought.
She manhandles boxes in a lift, tripping into the copier room,
bending to hide the two tubs on a thick red rug.

The soon-to-be-somethings sit between the bulky, hot machines,
tupperware tickling the cramped desert of the backroom.
She longs for them all to burst open – supernovae in the office – alive!
As long as you can make frogs happen, do it. No more dry planets.

No dry lips.

The Average Woman

the average woman earns   an average
woman   is capable of   average failure
is a product of   average women   is a type
of potent woman   is an average attempt of
branding women   an average family is
war against the average woman   warned
against promise   the average optimism
of sheer average   the average woman
is a promise   is blank energy   masturbatory
a cliff face   so average   energy   average
wanking away the average   the average blame
shameful behaviour   the shame is average
the average woman   is ashamed   looking up
at average ceiling tiles   the average body
is a coffin   is an average coffin   blames
the average woman   is a coffin   is ashamed
is disappointed   average   ever average

Lamb

All I ever wanted was to see your face

LAMB 'ZERO'

all I have is notes
scraps I send myself

how badly I want to write
how bad the words come out

I try to reassure myself, touch
paper with the tip of my thumb

be here with me, please
touch my thumb to my lips

Making Kim-Joy's Recipe for Multicoloured Shortbread Buttons

> There is no more fruitful source of family discontent than
> a housewife's badly cooked dinners and untidy ways.
>
> MRS BEETON

these make great gifts
take care in the fire
beat together, beat again
these make great gifts
make fire while the fire shines
stamp out simple circles
use a smaller cutter
these make fierce gifts
the tougher it will be
necessary, threatening
beat again, until firm enough
these make great flames
fight fire with fire
start acting fierce
stamp out everything
fire makes a great gift

Aphra the Destroyer

libretto for Matt

I am Aphra the Destroyer.
Look! I've got your nose!
I have scab-treasures, sock-demons, spider-trophies.
Beware my flying mandarins of fire!
I am hair-shaper, bone-twister, flesh-burner.
I am here for your heart.
I am slave-caller, book-eater, hell-master, blood-licker,
pall-caster, gut-splitter, death-sculptor.
My halls are lined with bones.
Bury me with my sword of foam.
Look into my eyes, my darling, my darling.
There's nothing there.

III

Ease myself into a body bag

PJ HARVEY, *'Plants and Rags'*

LIEBE

at Murnau's 1922 silent film Faust *performed with a live orchestra*

1

Drums roll. We settle. Shadows
of the dead hunt over the Earth.
Horses breathe fire, bearing skeletons.
The Devil says, 'The Earth is mine.'
Plague falls across the land.
Crowds cry: 'We still live!
We still love! We shall all die
dancing in each other's arms!'
No one is listening to anyone.
No one cares about anyone.
Faust burns his books. The Bible
burns best. Here is grinning Death,
seducing you. Mephisto as voyeur.
Mephisto, new pornographer. 'You
have tasted all of life's pleasures!
What is it that you want?'

2

Every villager carries a flower.
A white bridge is filled with horses
wearing bridles, bearing blossoms.
A girl with golden plaits kisses
her mother. Now life stands still.
'All is as it was.' Her Bible falls
at Faust's feet. He picks it up
and gives it back to her.
Faust's face is a discovery.
'She is not for you.' The pious girl
is hurrying away. 'I want only her.'
Your hand is on my knee and
I'm sorry I am scribbling.
Faust looks towards the light.
Mephisto understands
something of torture.

3

'Good gracious, how pretty
you are!' The girl smiles.
'Any lovers yet?' The girl
sees Mephisto's golden chain,
and does not hide. This gold
marks something new she wants.
Outside the window, Faust.
In her thoughts, only Faust.
'Any lovers yet?' The girl
desires fresh air. To breathe.
Discoveries will not subside.
She turns and torture catches
in her face. We watch the screen.
She picks the golden necklace up,
drapes it across her chest.
I hold my breath, uncross my legs.

4

Lick your lips. Auntie has come
home. An aside, an old debauch,
cautionary, lapping at a love potion.
Mephisto dances a string
of gold coins around her neck.
Auntie's coarse face delights
as he fastens it with lust,
reaching up under her arms
to smooth the money down
over her wide flat breasts
and holds them there.
Her hands search down
over thick skirts, below
her waist, pushing in,
her fingers an inverted prayer,
pushing the prayer further in.

5

Children play in the grass.
The girl is chased by Faust.
But. She wears the necklace.
She walks a stair of flowers
and plucks their petals bare.
LIEBT MICH. LIEBT MICH
NICHT. Faust falls to his knees.
'Yes, with all his heart
he loves you,' Faust insists.
Nothing else exists. They lock
and unlock each other in a kiss.
What is it that you want?
Darkness provides its own
intimacy. Now. Your hand
on the page I am writing.
Your eyes on my words.

6

The girl unbraids her hair in bed,
alone, as Mephisto approaches
the quiet house. She thinks of Faust.
Shivers. It is, basically, a love story.
Faust puts his palms against the glass.
Faust pushes against her waist.
Faust forces his way in. Cold
and death-like her arm reaches up
and drags him down into her face.
A tempest builds in the mouth of
Mephisto. He gathers Faust and flees.
The girl is left alone. The girl weeps.
Nothing is as it was. Everything is shame,
and in shame now she has a name: Gretchen.
'Touch me not, harlot.' We are all dead
like her. Our lips won't last forever.

7

The snow is possible. Snow falls.
A child is possible. Shame has not
meant the death of possibility.
She weeps dark tears in real snow.
Snow falls. Love. Gretchen
has snow in her eyes. Her tears
turn to frost. She tries to warm
her child. Here there is no sleep.
Through the ice she sees a cradle
in the snow, made of snow, ice.
She puts the baby in the cradle
in the snow, made of snow, ice.
We see the snow boy of winter
cry. We see him sleep. He dies.
Gretchen's face runs white with frost.
The snow falls deep around them.

8

Men come as they always do,
with spears. The frost Madonna
screams in violins, in mountains,
frozen trees alive with scream,
her face wide with only scream.
Now only the scream is possible.
Faust stands in the grey mist silent,
startled by the terror of her face.
'Mephisto! You have betrayed me!'
Gretchen suffers serenely, dreaming.
She sees grass and other children
picking flowers for a sweetheart.
In her frozen cell she tilts up her face,
to us, waiting for a kiss. Men
outside prepare her stake, packing wood,
branches, leaves around its base.

9

Faust finds her funeral pyre.
The match is struck. Fire lit.
We all lean forward in our seats.
Faust reaches Gretchen, wills
her eyes to open. Two faces,
heedless of age or doubt,
understand one another. This
is discovery. This is your face.
There are no words. There are
no words. Only a kiss is possible.
Time rushes with forgiveness.
Black smoke envelops them
and there is joy in death,
joy in the correct farewell.
With the blissful death of sin,
true life can once again begin.

10

An angel comes at last to chase
Mephisto off with a single word.
'The word that wings joyfully
throughout the universe, the word
that appeases every pain and grief,
the word that expiates all guilt,
the eternal word.' Now is the time
for violins, for tears, unburdening.
Every flicker on the screen is joy,
flares of joy in black and white,
a word of light, the only cold reality
tonight: LIEBE. The lights come on
to silence. A pause before the clapping
starts. Soon we will be bound for home
in silence. The air is grey. It hangs
with everything we do not want to say.

IV

Don't get any big ideas / They're not gonna happen

RADIOHEAD, *'Big Ideas (Don't Get Any)'*

O Goat Moon

And everything with wings is restless, aimless, drunk and dour

JOANNA NEWSOM, 'Emily'

O to regain control and find my feet
* now everything's shifting underneath.*
Ball bearings on the floor steal one thigh
* away, jar my hand, pull my shoulder*
down, down to the ground and on my knees.

O to regain some calm in the rainslicked
* guiltblocked, flawless flatpacked streets*
of Southwark. O Goat Moon I'm here.
* No one will know anything and I'm here.*
* You can show me anything. I'm here.*

The peace garden has heavy doors,
    unfamiliar flowers, wire mesh walls
which fend off other realities, earthquakes.
    There was an earthquake in London once,
Reece told me, but he couldn't find anyone else
    who felt it. The invisible earth shakes
over and over. Concrete hearts tremble.

In a garden there is no need for possessions.
    What passes between us is the language
of air. The language of air speaks in desire,
    with no words and no silences. Mouth,
the air runs chaos against your cheek,
    full of love, whether you are aware
or not: nothing can defend against its kiss.

O to relinquish ciphers, see a pigeon
*   and to draw no meaning from it,*
other than a pigeon. O for singular
*   expression. No more minds in horseplay*
posing as experimental conversation.

O to kill connection, kill each sequence
*   scratched by feet and orange shrapnelled*
beaks: it's not divine communication.
*   Goat Moon, I know you are a lad of fire.*
*   Goat Moon, Goat Moon, we are liars.*

The bus reads COSMOS at St. George's Circus.
    The world opens at its feet and swallows
everything like a word, everything like a dead word.
    All words are dead weight if we throat them.
Drift through circus streets and look into the eye
    of Charlie Chaplin, pigeons up top, swarming.
See his dead stars, his lost dog, his door with a lock.

Paint the future white, off-white, dare you. If you
    cannot solve a problem here then cover it,
hover over streets, towers, the river, weaves of links,
    until the right solution has appeared. Paint the sky
cold and white, delineate your borders with a sigh:
    to the south, a phallic lipstick elephant calling,
to the north, the river running days towards the sea.

O to make up my mind and take a stand,
*   learn to keep my hands deep in my pockets,*
bend memory to will and resolution, ignore
*   each grim-faced heart's convulsion. Smile, fake.*
Goat Moon, O my Goat Moon, it's more than I can take.

O to steer the future off this track, pull back, back
out, crash through Embankment parks and make
the pavement swell with silence till it breaks apart.
Goat Moon, jettison our hearts in crates.
Goat Moon, it's too late.

I like to play Russian Roulette at night
    with an iPod shuffle and Joanna Newsom
is a bullet. I watch graffiti under Thames bridges,
    the painting-over, impulses to write, rewrite,
as tides huff and crawl, covering footprints in sand,
    in mud. Everything changes at different speeds
and lust coats everything in dust, these eyes, these streets.

Throat everything now, now sing. Let your chest
    bell ring silence. Swallow it all down, this life.
Maturity wreaks havoc and river wrecks lie sunk
    beneath the surface. There were cities here.
There were many things here which cannot resurface.
    Why does it feel that everything is a covering over?
Or seem to feel? Or seem to only, because it does?

    Here, as ever, there is never enough time.
    Here is where we build our house.
    Here is where we fall into the flat lands.

V

I don't know. Who does know?

BEASTIE BOYS, *'I Don't Know'*

LA Story

a hot dog flies
over the hills of Hollywood
an endless gesture, a tired clown

    let your mind go
    and your body will follow

learn to laugh
learn to be happy
learn how to predict the weather

Improv

What isn't said isn't known. No one can read between the lines when there are none. You don't need to be obvious, just be clear. Remember, you are always communicating.

Magic Kingdom

The business of mice is serious.

Not everyone wears pants.

Barf up your pain, a pineapple.

Wear the ears. Laugh.

Improv

So much communication is physical. Learn
to read other people's signals. Do not fear
your partner's eye contact. Even silence
can be listened to.

Moon Illusion

unruly city, great lit face
low behind tall palms,
    flamingo taco trucks

death perches on my shoulder
small feathers, a smile
    beaked in black

I know now, as she nods to me,
there is nothing, nothing left
    to worry about

Improv

Look out for shiny things that are unusual. Be specific. See what works and follow it into a pattern. Rest the game so it has more impact when you play it. The cardinal sin is being boring.

At Griffith Observatory

If all mankind could look through that telescope, it would
change the world

GRIFFITH J. GRIFFITH

Hey, it's all over – the world ended!

JAMES DEAN, *Rebel Without a Cause*

I look into the night sky
and see a star,
increasingly bright.

I would like some dirt please
do you have some dirt?

If I stand in the place
where stories happen
I become part of the fiction,
my body photographed from all angles,
our faces interchangeable.

please now, bring me some dirt

As the star approaches
the weather will change.
The great polar fields will rot.
The seas will warm.
The great people of the world
will look on.

please bring me some dirt now
bring me some dirt

We will disappear into blackness.
Even you will disappear.
We will disappear into the space
from which we came,
destroyed as we began,
in a burst of gas and fire.

dirt, now. I want some dirt

In all the immaturity of our universe
the Earth will not be missed.
Just one story in a billion
with an ending.

Improv

Commit to your character. Make bold choices. Don't be scared of big emotions. This isn't a normal day. This is the day something finally happens.

Sunset and La Brea

Driving on, Gerry told me the Chaplin
studios off Sunset and La Brea were
taken over by Henson who superimposed
a Kermit head where Charlie Chaplin's
used to be, which I took to mean that
everything is ephemeral, including our
systems for attributing worth, meaning
and reputation, you know, LA was a
desert once, the Grand Canyon wasn't
always a canyon, and what happens when
you turn the sprinklers off, turn the
sprinklers on, and I watched that video
about being turned into a tree after you
die, no matter what happened in your
personal life, though they say cremation is
more practical, but what is practical, really,
and I wonder at what point in human
history the dead started to outnumber
the living, pretty quickly I guess, with
survival of the fittest, still, I like being
alive in a time of muppets, as the world
goes on changing, and who wouldn't
want to fall in love with everything, to
reach a hand out the window as it all
breezes past?

Improv

Surrender yourself to this moment. Learn to be spontaneous. The best way to avoid being afraid is to pretend you are someone who is not afraid. React to what is happening. If this is true, what else is true?

Yellow Reflection

Are we all small
clowns at heart, out of costume,
weeping banana peels?

Improv

Accept mistakes as gifts. Don't ignore them. You don't need to force them. You don't need to be afraid of them. You can choose how much of yourself to reveal. You can choose whether to use your losses.

VI

"   "

FLEETWOOD MAC, *'Albatross'*

Dimpsy

Light was just a trick
and night is coming on.
Hush. Adjust your eyes
to the new monochrome,
this world becoming
grey, grey in all things,
a stunning grey where
the world still turns;
the sky reveals its depths
in the expanding dark,
our own quiet smallness;
and where, at any moment,
drowsy sleepers not yet
lost to gathering night,
if suddenly awakened,
all might burst into song.

Holdfasts

Horses hide in kelp forests,
brushing past barbed arms
of a bract lagoon. They're
missing something. Warmth.
Dragons cold as clouds,
in currents washing back
and forth in blue wrack,
in sway, in undulating pods.
No heat. No possible fire.
Light embers die in depths
cut by sand, hope drained
while dragon horses sleep.
Years seem to pass. Longing.
Withdrawn in dragon silence.
Nothing happens, nothing
happens. Till the sky, way off,
a different strata of light,
changes. Darkness sparks
overhead and black weight
crawls deep into the body.
Now motion is unavoidable.
Holdfasts. Storm is coming.

Introduction to Charts

write your own responses as the poem is spoken

⊙

a chart will give you information on dangers
as well as enabling you to plot your position
and your intended course going forwards

a chart is essentially a flat diagram of the Earth's surface
but, as the Earth's surface is not flat, a projection must be used
this projection is then overlaid with imaginary lines

tell me, what in your life do you feel
most grateful for?

she told me not to 'go crazy', be good, to
smile for the camera, just so, just so
I could smile in comfort, not like that,
do my best, I am so comfortable, so
where is that memory that haunts me,
where is my trigger, my little trial, my
quiet mouse ears in a dark room,
the darkness which seems to settle under
everything, palm trees waving, throwing
everything away beyond the stars

⊙

different types of obstruction are noted by symbols
rocks which are never covered over by the sea, rocks
which both cover and uncover, underwater rocks

the depths of which are unknown but which are
considered unsuitable for surface navigation
reefs, breakers, wrecks, posts, piles and foul areas

tell me, if you could change anything about
the way you were raised, what would it be?

tough, tough, you ask too much, it's up to me,
I don't believe in miracles, I don't have to say it
or tell you anything, words begin in nothing,
everyone has a unique point of view, if this is
true, what else is true, who decides about truth,
how someone made me and I think, I want release
the pressure builds around my neck you know
I feel, it never feels, I never scream except
alone at night into the dark silence silently

☉

the seabed's composition is noted where known
the more unusual types being coral, kelp, ooze,
quartz, madrepore, basalt, lava, pumice and tuta

tell me, what is your most terrible memory?

something about the ceiling, looking up,
and the door open in the corner, no sky,
people passing by, the way those tiles could
lift up with a fingertip, could chip and fall
enter my mouth as the darkness takes me,
the door wide open and people passing by
and no one is thinking about me at all

⊙

coastlines may be surveyed or unsurveyed
both are indicated by a different type of line, as are
cliffs, hillocks, swamps, and sandy and stony shores

tell me, when was the last time you cried
in front of another person?

no one told me it was going to be like this
no one talks about confusion because it's
a dead end, narratively speaking, are you
the sort of protagonist who, are you even
anyone's protagonist, the woman who risked
nothing, who made no choice to lose but
kept on losing, it kept on happening,
let the lifetime build up like a shaken can,
don't spare a drop, don't drink tears, ask
mother if you can drink other people's tears

⊙

cultural features are noted as points of reference
urban areas, settlements, ruins, ruined landmarks,
chimneys, wind farms, radio towers and military installations

tell me, of all the people in your family, whose
death would you find the most disturbing?

what are you asking me, am I asking myself,
how can you ask this plainly it is not the old,
must be the young, the younger the more
painful, but how far does that go? how many
years old, months, weeks? when does grief begin?
when does the tap turn off for the glass just
drizzled with eternal life? this isn't life, this is
the end of life, the end of lies, no maps,
no bicycles, my thumb in my mouth, the bird,
the deaths, all the birds in the garden, waiting

⊙

harbour entrances are marked with a system of buoys
they can vary in size, construction and colour
they are generally shaped like a bell or barrel

green or black buoys must be kept to starboard
single colour red, yellow or orange buoys must be kept to port
special buoys or isolated danger marks are denoted with a bespoke symbol

tell me, what is the greatest accomplishment of your life?

what would you consider to be a great accomplishment?
I sailed across an ocean once? I have accomplished some
things? I don't know that they're any greater than the similar
accomplishments of other people around me? I suppose
it's all relative though? there have been days when just
getting out of bed, washing and dressing myself, feels like
a great accomplishment? why will no one tell me? what is
going to happen? I keep thinking I have some tangible
hold on where I am in my life and who I am, but really
I am just here in this moment, in this one, in this one

☉

pilotage is the skill of navigating in confined waters
you must use various means to track your position
carefully avoiding all hazards in the area

it can be difficult to identify landmarks you are looking for
mistakes are easily made especially when you are tired
beware of seeing only what you want to see

now tell me your life story. use as much detail as possible

Stingray Gambit

15:07^{03} People line around the low, lidless tank
with their hands half dipped in, waiting
for stingless rays to swim beneath and graze
their tentative fingertips. 15:07^{26} A few pass
and though I feel desire to touch I fear
new sensations. 15:07^{37} The mottle turns
15:07^{42} and she comes to me. It is as a friend
might do, and I feel compelled to respond. 15:07^{49}
I breathe, and slip my hand down to touch her.
She's soft under my fingers, not quite tough,
just old and fibrous, rippling to my tips,
so real, so far beyond my imagination.
I cannot photograph this, but I can 15:07^{51}
pull my hand back up: glistening, wet, new.